D1625435

A LIFE
of
GRATITUDE

we can
only be said
to be alive
in those
moments
when our hearts
are conscious
of our
treasures.
-THORNTON WILDER

A LIFE
of
GRATITUDE

*A Journal to Appreciate It All,
Big and Small*

LORI ROBERTS

CHRONICLE BOOKS
SAN FRANCISCO

Copyright © 2018 by Lori Roberts.
All rights reserved. No part of this book may be reproduced in any
form without written permission from the publisher.

ISBN 978-1-4521-6431-1

Manufactured in China

MIX
Paper from
responsible sources
FSC
www.fsc.org
FSC™ C136333

10 9 8 7 6 5 4

Chronicle books and gifts are available at special quantity discounts
to corporations, professional associations, literacy programs, and
other organizations. For details and discount information, please
contact our corporate/premiums department at corporatesales@
chroniclebooks.com or at 1-800-759-0190.

Chronicle Books LLC
680 Second Street
San Francisco, California 94107
www.chroniclebooks.com

It's easy to focus on all the stresses, problems, and nuisances in our lives: daily chores, rush-hour traffic, politics. At some point I noticed how much of my time was consumed with grumbling and negative thoughts, so I started an experiment in mindfulness and gratitude. I focused more on appreciating the little things in my life and seeing more of the positive instead of the negative. It was a subtle shift in my outlook, but over time I began to see the world through a new lens of awareness. That's what this journal is all about—choosing to notice the good stuff more often, to reflect on what is positive, helpful, amazing, and joyous in our lives. You can't always choose joy, just as you can't always ignore bad things in the world or negative feelings. But you can train your brain to think more positively by adopting a readiness to show appreciation for the littlest things.

This journal can be used as often as you want and on no particular schedule. Think about what time of day you might be more likely to write—in the morning before you start your day, or in bed as you reflect on the day's events? And remember that regular journal entries will help train your brain to start seeing gratitude all around you. Make it a habit, and let it be an opportunity to notice the often-overlooked blessings you already have and hopefully brighten your perspective on life.

BEGIN NOW

Start wherever you are right now. Pause and really look around. What do you appreciate and why?

_____

_____

_____

_____

_____

_____

_____

_____

_____

_____

_____

_____

_____

_____

_____

_____

_____

_____

_____

_____

_____

ORDINARY THINGS

Five ordinary things I am thankful for today:

1

2

3

4

5

MAKE A HABIT OF GRATITUDE

How will you develop a habit of gratitude? What will that habit look like, and what do you hope to gain from it?

_____

_____

_____

_____

_____

_____

_____

_____

_____

_____

_____

_____

It isn't always easy to remember our strengths, the good things about ourselves. Instead we focus on the bad stuff: I'm not good in social situations. I need to lose twenty pounds. My kneecaps are ugly. But those negative thoughts do not define us and often aren't even accurate reflections of what others see. We each have personality traits that are really awesome!

Ten wonderful things about me:

1 _____

2 _____

3 _____

4 _____

5 _____

6 _____

7 _____

8 _____

9 _____

10 _____

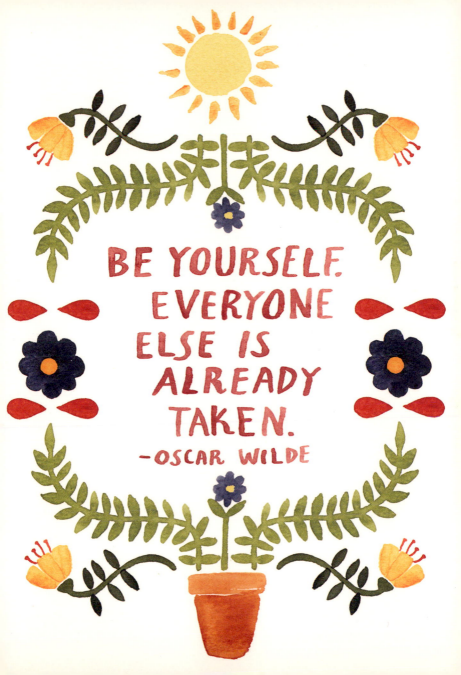

After a long winter, spring is surely welcomed with open arms: budding trees, early flowers, and more sunlight. What do you appreciate about spring?

_____

_____

_____

_____

_____

_____

_____

_____

_____

_____

_____

_____

_____

_____

_____

_____

_____

_____

_____

_____

A SPRING PROJECT: GROW HERBS ON YOUR WINDOWSILL

SENSE OF TOUCH

An electric blanket on a chilly night, a warm embrace, a barefoot walk in the grass—there are so many ways to experience touch. Every once in a while, stop and think about this sensation. What are your favorite things to touch?

_____

_____

_____

_____

_____

_____

_____

_____

_____

_____

_____

_____

_____

_____

_____

_____

_____

_____

_____

_____

_____

Think about a pet you have now or had in the past, or a friend's pet that you have loved playing with. What does this animal mean to you? Why are you thankful to have this pet in your life?

Until one has loved an animal,

a part of one's soul remains unawakened.

—ANATOLE FRANCE

RED

How does the color red make you feel? What are some of your favorite red things?

_____

_____

_____

_____

_____

_____

_____

_____

_____

_____

_____

_____

_____

_____

_____

_____

_____

For everything there is a season. As one season changes to the next, take a moment to reflect on what change means to you. Each season has a purpose. Each time in our lives has a purpose. Think about who you are now compared with who you were in the past, and envision what lies ahead.

_____

_____

_____

_____

_____

_____

_____

_____

_____

_____

_____

_____

_____

_____

_____

_____

_____

_____

_____

_____

How do you spend your free time? Do you have a favorite hobby or pastime? Are you a sci-fi movie fanatic, do you play tennis every weekend, or do you prefer curling up with a good book? How do your hobbies improve your quality of life? What brings you joy?

_____

_____

_____

_____

_____

_____

_____

_____

_____

_____

_____

_____

_____

_____

_____

_____

_____

_____

_____

FLIP IT

We can complain about our jobs, or we can rejoice in receiving a steady paycheck. We can gripe about having to empty the dishwasher, or we can celebrate having a dishwasher and having hot water come directly into the house. Take some things you usually gripe about and flip them to something positive:

_____

_____

_____

_____

_____

_____

_____

_____

_____

_____

_____

_____

_____

_____

_____

_____

_____

_____

_____

_____

_____

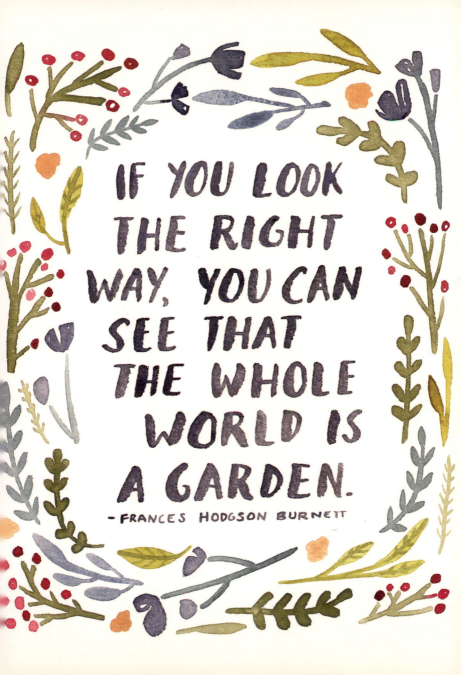

IF YOU LOOK
THE RIGHT
WAY, YOU CAN
SEE THAT
THE WHOLE
WORLD IS
A GARDEN.
-FRANCES HODGSON BURNETT

PROJECT: GIVE THANK-YOU NOTES

Make a list of people you think are overdue for a thank-you: the mail carrier who makes sure your magazines don't get crumpled, the coworker who always brings homemade cookies to the office, or the neighbor who checks on your goldfish when you're on vacation.

Five people I plan to give thank-you notes to and why:

1 _____

_____

2 _____

_____

3 _____

_____

4 _____

_____

5 _____

_____

_____

IF THE ONLY PRAYER
YOU EVER SAY IN
YOUR WHOLE LIFE
IS
"THANK YOU,"
THAT WOULD
SUFFICE.

—MEISTER ECKHART

MORNING RITUAL

Do you have a morning routine? Do you like to enjoy a cup of coffee or watch the news after waking up? Why not start with gratitude to set the tone for the rest of the day?

Write down some ideas here for a new morning ritual rooted in gratitude and mindfulness:

_____

_____

_____

_____

_____

_____

_____

_____

_____

_____

_____

_____

OUT-OF-THE-ORDINARY THINGS

Five out-of-the-ordinary things I am thankful for today:

1

2

3

4

5

WRITE A LETTER

Write a letter to someone from your past—a teacher, coach, friend—who influenced you and helped you become the person you are today. What did they do that stands out to you? How did that make you feel? Why are you thankful that they were a part of your life? What do you want to make sure they know?

_____

_____

_____

_____

_____

_____

_____

_____

_____

_____

_____

_____

_____

_____

_____

_____

_____

_____

blessed is the influence of one true, loving human soul on another.

-GEORGE ELIOT

Whether it's roller-skating, making a mean gumbo, competitive latte art, or something else entirely, what are some talents that you're proud of?

_____

_____

_____

_____

_____

_____

_____

_____

_____

_____

_____

_____

_____

_____

_____

_____

_____

_____

_____

Today is a great day because:

_____
_____
_____
_____
_____
_____
_____
_____
_____
_____
_____
_____
_____
_____
_____
_____
_____
_____
_____
_____

FAVORITE MEMORIES

What are your favorite childhood memories? List some of them here:

_____

_____

_____

_____

_____

_____

_____

_____

_____

_____

_____

_____

_____

_____

_____

_____

_____

_____

_____

_____

_____

MAKING A LIVING

Do you have a job? Full-time, part-time? Whether it's your dream job, unpaid work, or just something to pay the bills, or even if you're between jobs, what are some things you value about your employment situation right now? How can you find gratitude in the current stage of your career?

ORANGE

How does the color orange make you feel? What are some of your favorite orange things?

_____

_____

_____

_____

_____

_____

_____

_____

_____

_____

_____

_____

_____

_____

_____

_____

_____

count your
joys
instead of
your woes.
Count your
friends
instead of your
foes. —IRISH
PROVERB

Joys I am grateful for today:

_____

_____

_____

_____

_____

_____

_____

_____

_____

_____

_____

_____

_____

_____

_____

_____

_____

_____

_____

_____

_____

_____

IN THE NAME OF LOVE

In a sea of to-dos, work woes, and daily struggles, it's easy to slip into auto-pilot and forget to say "thank you" to that person (or people) in your life who helps you make it all happen. Start a list here of things you love, value, and appreciate about that someone (or those someones):

_____

_____

_____

_____

_____

_____

_____

_____

_____

_____

_____

_____

_____

_____

_____

_____

_____

_____

_____

_____

_____

_____

IT TAKES A VILLAGE

Think about parenting—how you were parented, and if you have children, how you parent your own kids. In your life, what have you learned about parenting? What aspects of parenting are you most grateful for?

_____

_____

_____

_____

_____

_____

_____

_____

_____

_____

_____

_____

_____

_____

_____

_____

_____

_____

_____

_____

_____

HOME SWEET HOME

Wherever we live—city apartment, country cabin, suburban ranch—our homes are our safe havens, our sanctuaries. What do you love and appreciate about your home? What kind of home do you envision having in the future?

_____

_____

_____

_____

_____

_____

_____

_____

_____

_____

_____

_____

_____

_____

_____

_____

_____

_____

_____

_____

_____

_____

_____

_____

Books have the power to transport us to faraway places or change the way we see and relate to the world. Some of us even credit a book for changing our lives. What books are you grateful for or what books have shaped the person you've become? What is special about them?

_____

_____

_____

_____

_____

_____

_____

_____

_____

_____

_____

_____

_____

_____

_____

_____

_____

_____

_____

_____

_____

MORNING MINDFULNESS

Begin each day with a grateful heart. The next time you wake up, stay in bed for a moment. Lie still, close your eyes, and think about the possibilities of the new day ahead of you.

Ten things I am grateful for this morning:

1 _____

2 _____

3 _____

4 _____

5 _____

6 _____

7 _____

8 _____

9 _____

10 _____

The human body is an amazing thing. Consider how awesome it is that our brains give us the ability to form opinions and emotions, and how cool it is that our vocal cords let us talk to one another. How incredible is it that we have hands? And opposable thumbs? What do you love that your body can do? What are you grateful for?

_____

_____

_____

_____

_____

_____

_____

_____

_____

_____

_____

_____

_____

_____

_____

_____

_____

_____

_____

Things I find beautiful today:

_____
_____
_____
_____
_____
_____
_____
_____
_____
_____
_____
_____
_____
_____
_____
_____
_____
_____
_____
_____

SENSE OF TASTE

Your mom's famous banana bread, super-spicy pad Thai, a refreshing glass of water after eating super-spicy pad Thai—there are so many wonderful things to taste. Every once in a while, think about this sensation. List your favorite tastes here:

_____

_____

_____

_____

_____

_____

_____

_____

_____

_____

_____

_____

_____

_____

_____

_____

_____

_____

_____

_____

WATER IS LIFE

Not only do we need water for survival, but also we are inherently drawn to it—oceans, rivers, even swimming pools. Think about water in all its forms: in the coffee we drink, in the sauna we enjoy, in the waterfalls we photograph. Consider how nice it is to have water pumped directly into our homes! What do you appreciate about water?

_____

_____

_____

_____

_____

_____

_____

_____

_____

_____

_____

_____

_____

_____

_____

_____

_____

_____

_____

NIGHTTIME MINDFULNESS

End the day with gratitude by reflecting on the day's events and focusing on your well-spent moments.

Top ten things about today:

1 _____

2 _____

3 _____

4 _____

5 _____

6 _____

7 _____

8 _____

9 _____

10 _____

YELLOW

How does the color yellow make you feel? What are some of your favorite yellow things?

_____

_____

_____

_____

_____

_____

_____

_____

_____

_____

_____

_____

_____

_____

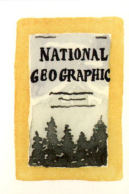

NATIONAL
GEOGRAPHIC

Are you currently experiencing a conflict or challenge in your life? Maybe you have a coworker you don't care for, or you're having financial difficulties. Challenge yourself to find the positive side of the experience. Write about it here:

_____

_____

_____

_____

_____

_____

_____

_____

_____

_____

_____

_____

_____

_____

_____

_____

_____

_____

_____

_____

_____

_____

_____

LITTLE COMFORTS

Modern life is filled with little things that make our lives easier or more comfortable—spell-check, toilet paper, scissors, toenail clippers, silverware. Brainstorm a list of little conveniences that you are thankful for here:

AMAZING EARTH

Pretty complex and amazing things are happening all around us, and we hardly even notice! Tiny acorns turn into huge trees, bees pollinate our flowers and food, phytoplankton produces 50 percent of the earth's oxygen. What miracles in nature do you appreciate?

_____

_____

_____

_____

_____

_____

_____

_____

_____

_____

_____

_____

_____

_____

_____

_____

_____

_____

_____

_____

With longer days and warmer temperatures, we have more opportunities to play outside. The supermarket is overflowing with the season's fruits and vegetables, and our patio flowers are in full bloom. What do you appreciate about summer?

_____

_____

_____

_____

_____

_____

_____

_____

_____

_____

_____

_____

_____

_____

_____

_____

_____

_____

_____

_____

A SUMMER PROJECT: MAKE FRUIT POPSICLES

Art affects us in ways we can't always understand. And it's everywhere—in museums, stuck to the fridge, spray-painted on train cars, plastered on billboards, painted on shop windows. What kind of art do you appreciate and why? How does it move you? Extra credit: Make a piece of art that represents your gratitude for something.

_____

_____

_____

_____

_____

_____

_____

_____

_____

_____

_____

_____

_____

_____

_____

_____

_____

_____

_____

_____

_____

THE ESSENCE OF ALL BEAUTIFUL ART, ALL GREAT ART, IS GRATITUDE.

-FRIEDRICH NIETZSCHE

_____

_____

_____

_____

_____

_____

_____

_____

_____

_____

_____

_____

_____

_____

_____

_____

_____

_____

_____

GREEN

How does the color green make you feel? What are some of your favorite green things?

_____

_____

_____

_____

_____

_____

_____

_____

_____

_____

_____

_____

_____

_____

_____

_____

Joys I am grateful for today:

_____

_____

_____

_____

_____

_____

_____

_____

_____

_____

_____

_____

_____

_____

_____

_____

_____

_____

_____

_____

_____

FAVORITE MEMORIES

What are your favorite teenage memories? Write about some of them here:

_____

_____

_____

_____

_____

_____

_____

_____

_____

_____

_____

_____

_____

_____

_____

_____

_____

_____

_____

_____

_____

_____

_____

PROJECT: MAKE A GRATITUDE BULLETIN BOARD

Filling a bulletin board with visual reminders of your abundance—family, friends, a fantastic vacation, a cherished love note—is a quick and easy way to tap into some positive energy. What kinds of things will you include on your board? List them here:

_____

_____

_____

_____

_____

_____

_____

_____

_____

_____

_____

_____

_____

_____

_____

_____

_____

_____

_____

Watching the evening news can be depressing, as it can seem to focus on the darkness in the world. Think about the people who always show up for you in times of crisis. Brainstorm ways you would like to say "thank you" to people who help in your community or abroad. By making a donation to a charitable organization? By sending a short note of appreciation to your local fire station? Write some ideas here:

_____

_____

_____

_____

_____

_____

_____

_____

_____

_____

_____

_____

_____

_____

_____

_____

_____

_____

_____

We are the sum of the choices we make in our lives—some good, some not so good. It's easy to pat ourselves on the back when a choice we make turns out to be a good one, but it can be challenging to see the lesson when a decision we made might have led us astray. Look back on some of your life choices, both ones you're proud of and ones you might regret. What are the lessons you are grateful for?

_____

_____

_____

_____

_____

_____

_____

_____

_____

_____

_____

_____

_____

_____

_____

_____

_____

_____

Make peace with your past. Sometimes it's not our choice when something ends—a relationship, a job, a way of life. Think back on a situation that was out of your control and at the time seemed devastating. Is there anything about that situation that can be seen as positive? Even if you can't find something to be grateful for, consider doing something for yourself or someone else—an act of kindness—and dedicate this act of kindness to the world as a form of closure.

_____

_____

_____

_____

_____

_____

_____

_____

_____

_____

_____

_____

_____

_____

_____

_____

_____

_____

OUT-OF-THE-ORDINARY THINGS

Five out-of-the-ordinary things I am thankful for today:

1
_____
_____
_____

2
_____
_____
_____

3
_____
_____
_____

4
_____
_____
_____

5
_____
_____
_____

SENSE OF SMELL

Chocolate-chip cookies in the oven, lavender in the summertime, popcorn in a movie theater—there are so many wonderful smells. Every once in a while, close your eyes and take in the scents around you. List your favorite scents here:

_____

_____

_____

_____

_____

_____

_____

_____

_____

_____

_____

_____

_____

_____

_____

_____

_____

_____

_____

_____

_____

Think about where you live—your state, your town, your neighborhood. Do you have a favorite store you frequent? Does your mail carrier know your name? Does your neighbor have a beautiful garden for you to admire? What do you appreciate about where you live right now?

_____

_____

_____

_____

_____

_____

_____

_____

_____

_____

_____

_____

_____

_____

_____

_____

_____

_____

_____

KNOWLEDGE IS POWER

Life is full of opportunities to learn something new, and we pick up little bits of wisdom along the way. Think about what it means to learn, to be curious, to be amazed. What new abilities or perspectives have you gained in your life? Who has been your greatest teacher?

_____

_____

_____

_____

_____

_____

_____

_____

_____

_____

_____

_____

_____

_____

_____

_____

_____

_____

_____

_____

_____

I AM
STILL
LEARNING.

-MICHELANGELO,

age 87

CHANGE YOUR PERSPECTIVE: LOOK UP

Stand in a wide-open space—a park, a soccer field, your neighbor's driveway. Try it in the daytime and then again at night. What do you notice that you hadn't noticed before? What do you appreciate just by changing your vantage point?

_____

_____

_____

_____

_____

_____

_____

_____

_____

_____

_____

_____

_____

_____

_____

_____

_____

_____

_____

Things I find beautiful today:

_____
_____
_____
_____
_____
_____
_____
_____
_____
_____
_____
_____
_____
_____
_____
_____
_____

GRAY

How does the color gray make you feel? What are some of your favorite gray things?

_____

_____

_____

_____

_____

_____

_____

_____

_____

_____

_____

_____

_____

_____

_____

Science isn't just about chemistry experiments and space travel. Science is about exploration, curiosity, and learning. Think about how scientific advancements have affected you in your life—in the medical care you've received, in the energy you use to heat your home, in the food you eat. What do you appreciate about science?

_____

_____

_____

_____

_____

_____

_____

_____

_____

_____

_____

_____

_____

_____

_____

_____

_____

_____

_____

A LITTLE DISCOMFORT

Spiders. Jury duty. Taxes. These things might be necessary, but they're also uncomfortable for many and as a result are not always appreciated. What are some things you might not be too comfortable with but can find value in?

_____

_____

_____

_____

_____

_____

_____

_____

_____

_____

_____

_____

_____

_____

_____

_____

_____

_____

_____

_____

BLUE

How does the color blue make you feel? What are some of your favorite blue things?

_____

_____

_____

_____

_____

_____

_____

_____

_____

_____

_____

_____

_____

_____

_____

_____

Think about how helpful technology is in our daily lives—smartphones, flash drives, calculators, GPS, all at our fingertips. In what ways does technology make your life easier? What gadgets are you most grateful for?

_____

_____

_____

_____

_____

_____

_____

_____

_____

_____

_____

_____

_____

_____

_____

_____

_____

_____

_____

FAMILY TRADITIONS

How does your family celebrate holidays or milestones? Do you have a favorite birthday ritual or special recipe you cook on certain occasions? What family traditions are you grateful for?

_____

_____

_____

_____

_____

_____

_____

_____

_____

_____

_____

_____

_____

_____

_____

_____

_____

_____

_____

_____

Music can evoke powerful emotions. Close your eyes and listen to a favorite song—really listen. Why do you love it? How does it make you feel? Write down what you appreciate about your favorite music:

_____

_____

_____

_____

_____

_____

_____

_____

_____

_____

_____

_____

_____

_____

_____

_____

_____

_____

_____

_____

MORNING MINDFULNESS

The next time you wake up, stay in bed for a moment. Lie still, close your eyes, and think about the possibilities of the new day ahead of you.

Ten things I am grateful for this morning:

1 _____

2 _____

3 _____

4 _____

5 _____

6 _____

7 _____

8 _____

9 _____

10 _____

What are some of your most treasured possessions? A recipe from your great-aunt? A quilt that has been passed down for generations? A macaroni necklace from your child? List five of your most treasured possessions. Why are you grateful to have them?

_____

_____

_____

_____

_____

_____

_____

_____

_____

_____

_____

_____

_____

_____

_____

_____

_____

_____

_____

_____

_____

STOP AND SMELL THE ROSES

Sometimes we get so focused on a goal that we forget to enjoy the path along the way. What are three goals you are working toward right now? In what ways can you continue to strive for them but also be mindful of your current path? What do you appreciate about your journey so far?

_____

_____

_____

_____

_____

_____

_____

_____

_____

_____

_____

_____

_____

_____

_____

_____

_____

_____

_____

_____

_____

_____

Joys I am grateful for today:

_____
_____
_____
_____
_____
_____
_____
_____
_____
_____
_____
_____
_____
_____
_____
_____
_____
_____
_____

PURPLE

How does the color purple make you feel? What are some of your favorite purple things?

_____

_____

_____

_____

_____

_____

_____

_____

_____

_____

_____

_____

_____

_____

_____

_____

After a long, hot summer, some parts of the world are definitely ready for a reprieve. Picturesque fall colors, cooler temperatures, pumpkin-spice everything . . . What do you appreciate about fall?

_____

_____

_____

_____

_____

_____

_____

_____

_____

_____

_____

_____

_____

_____

_____

_____

_____

_____

WRITE A LETTER

Write a letter to someone in your present—your spouse, your partner, a family member, a friend—who is always there for you. How has this person changed your life for the better? How does he or she make you feel? Why are you thankful that he or she is a part of your life? What do you want to make sure this person knows?

_____

_____

_____

_____

_____

_____

_____

_____

_____

_____

_____

_____

_____

_____

_____

_____

_____

_____

_____

_____

_____

It can be difficult to reframe a situation in which we believe we have failed. But sometimes one door closes and another opens. What are some challenges you've overcome in your life? How did you pick yourself back up? What did you do to move on? Can you find any character-building lessons to be learned in this situation?

_____

_____

_____

_____

_____

_____

_____

_____

_____

_____

_____

_____

_____

_____

_____

_____

_____

_____

_____

OUR GREATEST GLORY IS, NOT IN NEVER FALLING, BUT IN RISING EVERY TIME WE FALL.
–OLIVER GOLDSMITH

BEHIND THE SCENES

Our world is filled with systems that make our lives a little bit easier: Our mail gets delivered, our garbage gets collected, our potholes get filled. Consider all the people in these systems who make the magic happen. List the people who make your life easier here:

_____

_____

_____

_____

_____

_____

_____

_____

_____

_____

_____

_____

_____

_____

_____

_____

_____

_____

_____

NIGHTTIME MINDFULNESS

End the day with gratitude by reflecting on the day's events and focusing on your well-spent moments.

Top ten things about today:

1 _____   6 _____

_____   _____

2 _____   7 _____

_____   _____

3 _____   8 _____

_____   _____

4 _____   9 _____

_____   _____

5 _____   10 _____

_____   _____

SENSE OF HEARING

Unbridled laughter, a cat's purr, a rushing river—there are so many wonderful sounds. Every once in a while, close your eyes and just listen. List your favorite sounds here:

_____

_____

_____

_____

_____

_____

_____

_____

_____

_____

_____

_____

_____

_____

_____

_____

_____

_____

_____

_____

_____

Think about a favorite vacation you've taken, whether it was halfway around the world or in a neighboring city. What do you enjoy about traveling? Meeting new people, trying new food, or turning off your phone and enjoying the silence? Recall some of your favorite vacations and write down what you appreciate about those experiences:

_____

_____

_____

_____

_____

_____

_____

_____

_____

_____

_____

_____

_____

_____

_____

_____

_____

_____

_____

_____

ORDINARY THINGS

Five ordinary things I am thankful for today:

1

2

3

4

5

EXTRA-
ORDINARY
MAGIC IS
WOVEN
THROUGH
ORDINARY
LIFE.

—AMY LEIGH MERCREE

PROJECT: HAVE A NO-ELECTRICITY DAY

There are some things in our lives that we are so used to having that they fade into the background, like electricity. Set aside a day, or even just an afternoon, and go without electricity. How did it feel to go without electric light, air conditioning, the radio, or TV? After noticing how different life is without these comforts, what do you appreciate about them?

_____

_____

_____

_____

_____

_____

_____

_____

_____

_____

_____

_____

_____

_____

_____

_____

_____

GRATITUDE BUCKET LIST

When we consider that we have a finite amount of time on this planet, we realize that every moment is a gift. Are you grateful for your health, your body, your two strong legs? Train for a 5K race. Do you love Latin music? Take up salsa dancing. Do you love Italian food? Plan a trip to Italy or take a deep dive into learning to cook your favorite dishes. Make a list and plot a course for gratitude in the future:

_____

_____

_____

_____

_____

_____

_____

_____

_____

_____

_____

_____

_____

_____

_____

_____

_____

_____

_____

_____

PINK

How does the color pink make you feel? What are some of your favorite pink things?

_____
_____
_____
_____
_____
_____
_____
_____
_____
_____
_____
_____
_____
_____
_____
_____

Pink Pearl

NIGHTTIME RITUAL

Do you have a nightly routine? Do you like to drink a cup of herbal tea or read a book before bed? Why not end the day by reflecting on the day's events? Write down some ideas here for a new bedtime ritual rooted in gratitude and mindfulness:

_____

_____

_____

_____

_____

_____

_____

_____

_____

_____

_____

_____

_____

_____

_____

_____

_____

_____

_____

You can't choose your family but you can choose your friends. Make a list here of the friends you have in your life. What do you appreciate about them? How do they enrich your life?

_____

_____

_____

_____

_____

_____

_____

_____

_____

_____

_____

_____

_____

_____

_____

_____

_____

_____

_____

_____

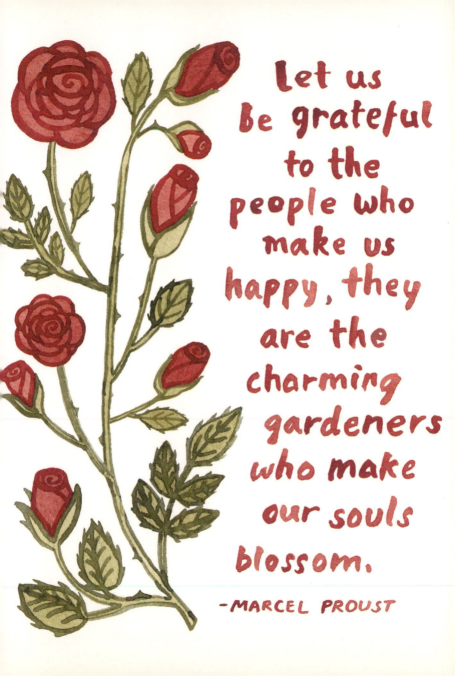

Let us
be grateful
to the
people who
make us
happy, they
are the
charming
gardeners
who make
our souls
blossom.

-MARCEL PROUST

LESSONS LEARNED

Every person from our past helped shape us into who we are today. Make a list of people who have most influenced you. Go beyond your supporters and consider those who challenged you as well. Why are you thankful for them? What lessons have you learned?

_____

_____

_____

_____

_____

_____

_____

_____

_____

_____

_____

_____

_____

_____

_____

_____

_____

_____

MORNING MINDFULNESS

The next time you wake up, stay in bed for a moment. Lie still, close your eyes, and think about the possibilities of the new day ahead of you.

Ten things I am grateful for this morning:

1 _____

_____

2 _____

_____

3 _____

_____

4 _____

_____

5 _____

_____

6 _____

_____

7 _____

_____

8 _____

_____

9 _____

_____

10 _____

_____

Things I find beautiful today:

_____
_____
_____
_____
_____
_____
_____
_____
_____
_____
_____
_____
_____
_____
_____
_____

BROWN

How does the color brown make you feel? What are some of your favorite brown things?

_____

_____

_____

_____

_____

_____

_____

_____

_____

_____

_____

_____

_____

_____

_____

_____

_____

_____

_____

FOOD FOR THOUGHT

For most of us, someone grows our food, picks it for us, and sells it to us. We have all kinds of gadgets that make food preparation a breeze. Consider your easy access to food and all the modern kitchen conveniences you enjoy. When you think about food, what are you thankful for?

_____

_____

_____

_____

_____

_____

_____

_____

_____

_____

_____

_____

_____

_____

_____

_____

_____

_____

_____

_____

TO-DO

There will always be ten thousand plates spinning in your life, a seemingly never-ending to-do list, a handful of problems to solve, people to call, errands to run. Pause. Reflect. Be present and thankful for this very moment. What are ten things you are thankful for right now?

1 _____

2 _____

3 _____

4 _____

5 _____

6 _____

7 _____

8 _____

9 _____

10 _____

Complaining about traffic is a common pastime. A better use of our time could be remembering how nice it is to have a car that runs or a top-notch public-transportation system that makes life easier. What modes of transportation do you use, and why are you thankful for them?

_____

_____

_____

_____

_____

_____

_____

_____

_____

_____

_____

_____

_____

_____

_____

_____

_____

_____

_____

_____

CHANGE YOUR PERSPECTIVE: LOOK DOWN

Get as close to the ground as you can. If you have a magnifying glass, now would be a great time to use it! What do you notice that you hadn't noticed before? What do you appreciate just by changing your vantage point?

_____

_____

_____

_____

_____

_____

_____

_____

_____

_____

_____

_____

_____

_____

_____

_____

_____

_____

_____

_____

Think about your heritage, your roots. Where does your family come from? Consider what it took your ancestors to get to this point. Did they immigrate from another country? What part of your family heritage are you most proud of?

_____

_____

_____

_____

_____

_____

_____

_____

_____

_____

_____

_____

_____

_____

_____

_____

_____

_____

_____

WHITE

How does the color white make you feel? What are some of your favorite white things?

_____

_____

_____

_____

_____

_____

_____

_____

_____

_____

_____

_____

_____

_____

_____

ORDINARY THINGS

Five ordinary things I am thankful for today:

1 _____
_____
_____

2 _____
_____
_____

3 _____
_____

4 _____
_____

5 _____
_____
_____

The shorter days of winter can be a time of hibernation, a time of renewal. Do you make soup and huddle around your woodstove, or are the temperatures mild where you live? What do you appreciate about winter?

_____

_____

_____

_____

_____

_____

_____

_____

_____

_____

_____

_____

_____

_____

_____

_____

_____

_____

_____

A WINTER PROJECT: MAKE BIRDSEED ORNAMENTS

PEARLS OF WISDOM

As we get older, we collect experiences that shape us. We learn things, we change, we adapt, we grow. At this point in your life, how do you feel about aging? What wisdom are you grateful to have accumulated so far?

_____

_____

_____

_____

_____

_____

_____

_____

_____

_____

_____

_____

_____

_____

_____

_____

_____

_____

_____

_____

_____

Not everyone is comfortable with being alone or being in silence. But being alone can actually help you recharge, focus, and discern and make room for gratitude. Spend a few minutes, or even an afternoon, alone and in silence. Allow yourself to simply be still with your thoughts and feelings of gratitude. How do you feel?

_____

_____

_____

_____

_____

_____

_____

_____

_____

_____

_____

_____

_____

_____

_____

_____

_____

_____

_____

_____

_____

WRITE A LETTER

Write a letter to someone you hope to have in your future—a child, a partner, a new friend. Think about things from your own life that you wish that you'd known sooner, as well as the positive things that encouraged you and how that they made you feel. What are things you're grateful for in your life that you would want to make sure this person knows?

SENSE OF SIGHT

A loved one you haven't seen in ages, a book from your childhood, the glow from a full moon casting shadows in the middle of the night—there are so many wonderful sights. Every once in a while, pause and really look around. List your favorite things to lay eyes on here:

_____

_____

_____

_____

_____

_____

_____

_____

_____

_____

_____

_____

_____

_____

_____

_____

_____

_____

_____

PROJECT: MAKE A GRATITUDE JAR

Jot down something every week (or every day, if you're ambitious!) that you are grateful for and add it to the jar. At the end of the year, read all the notes and celebrate your abundance.

_____

_____

_____

_____

_____

_____

_____

_____

_____

_____

_____

_____

_____

_____

_____

_____

_____

_____

_____

_____

_____

NIGHTTIME MINDFULNESS

End the day with gratitude by reflecting on the day's events and focusing on your well-spent moments.

Top ten things about today:

1 _____   6 _____

_____   _____

2 _____   7 _____

_____   _____

3 _____   8 _____

_____   _____

4 _____   9 _____

_____   _____

5 _____   10 _____

_____   _____

_____

BLACK

How does the color black make you feel? What are some of your favorite black things?

_____

_____

_____

_____

_____

_____

_____

_____

_____

_____

_____

_____

_____

_____

_____

_____

FAMILY TIES

Make a list of your family members here—siblings, grandparents, extended family. Why are you grateful for their presence in your life? If you have a difficult relationship with a family member, are there things about this person you can appreciate? Are there family members who have passed who helped shape who you are today?

_____

_____

_____

_____

_____

_____

_____

_____

_____

_____

_____

_____

_____

_____

_____

_____

_____

_____

_____

_____

_____

_____

_____

_____

_____

_____

_____

_____

_____

_____

_____

_____

_____

_____

_____

_____

FAVORITE MEMORIES

What are your favorite memories as an adult? List some of them here:

_____

_____

_____

_____

_____

_____

_____

_____

_____

_____

_____

_____

_____

_____

_____

_____

_____

_____

_____

_____

_____

_____

_____

_____

_____

Today is a great day because:

_____

_____

_____

_____

_____

_____

_____

_____

_____

_____

_____

_____

_____

_____

_____

_____

_____

_____